Air Fryer Cookbook for Two

Easy to make, Healthy and Delicious Air Fryer Recipes

Written By

Marion Bartolini

Table of Contents

INTRODUCTION

Thank you for purchasing this book!

Frying has become a bad word lately. As a result, we try to cut down on it in as many of our recipes as possible. Fortunately, air fryers are a great way to make food taste like it's been fried when it hasn't. So, here are some tips on cooking with air fryers:

Enjoy your reading!

BREAKFAST RECIPES

Veggie Burrito with Tofu

Preparation time: 10 minutes

Cooking time: 15 minutes

Servings: 8

Ingredients:

- 16 ounces tofu, crumbled
- 1 green bell pepper, chopped
- ¼ cup scallions, chopped
- 15 ounces canned black beans, drained
- 1 cup vegan salsa
- ½ cup water
- ¼ teaspoon cumin, ground
- ½ teaspoon turmeric powder
- ½ teaspoon smoked paprika
- A pinch of salt and black pepper
- ¼ teaspoon chili powder
- 3 cups spinach leaves, torn
- 8 vegan tortillas for serving

Directions:

1. In your air fryer, mix tofu with bell pepper, scallions, black beans, salsa, water, cumin, turmeric, paprika, salt, pepper and chili powder, stir, cover and cook at 370°f for 20 minutes

2. Add spinach, toss well, divide this on your vegan tortillas, roll, wrap them and serve for breakfast.
3. Enjoy!

Nutrition: Calories 211; Fat 4g; Fiber 7g; Carbs 14g; Protein 4g

Apple Steel Cut Oats

Preparation time: 10 minutes

Cooking time: 15 minutes

Servings: 6

Ingredients:

- 1 and ½ cups water
- 1 and ½ cups coconut milk
- 2 apples, cored, peeled and chopped
- 1 cup steel cut oats
- ½ teaspoon cinnamon powder
- ¼ teaspoon nutmeg, ground
- ¼ teaspoon allspice, ground
- ¼ teaspoon ginger powder
- ¼ teaspoon cardamom, ground
- 1 tablespoon flaxseed, ground
- 2 teaspoons vanilla extract
- 2 teaspoons stevia
- Cooking spray

Directions:

1. Spray your air fryer with cooking spray, add apples, milk, water, cinnamon, oats, allspice, nutmeg, cardamom, ginger, vanilla, flaxseeds and stevia, stir, cover and cook at 360°f for 15 minutes
2. Divide into bowls and serve for breakfast.
3. Enjoy!

Nutrition: Calories 172; Fat 3g; Fiber 7g; Carbs 8g; Protein 5g

Lemony Tofu Casserole

Preparation time: 10 minutes

Cooking time: 20 minutes

Servings: 4

Ingredients:

- 1 teaspoon lemon zest, grated
- 14 ounces tofu, cubed
- 1 tablespoon lemon juice
- 2 tablespoons nutritional yeast
- 1 tablespoon apple cider vinegar
- 1 tablespoon olive oil
- 2 garlic cloves, minced
- 10 ounces spinach, torn
- ½ cup yellow onion, chopped
- ½ teaspoon basil, dried
- 8 ounces mushrooms, sliced
- Salt and black pepper to the taste
- ¼ teaspoon red pepper flakes
- Cooking spray

Directions:

1. Spray your air fryer with some cooking spray, arrange tofu cubes on the bottom, add lemon zest, lemon juice, yeast, vinegar, olive oil, garlic, spinach, onion, basil, mushrooms, salt, pepper and pepper flakes, toss, cover and cook at 365°f for 20 minutes.
2. Divide between plates and serve for breakfast.
3. Enjoy!

Nutrition: Calories 246, Fat 6g; Fiber 8g; Carbs 12g; Protein 4g

Carrot Mix

Preparation time: 10 minutes

Cooking time: 15 minutes

Servings: 4

Ingredients:

- 2 cups coconut milk
- ½ cup steel cut oats
- 1 cup carrots, shredded
- 1 teaspoon cardamom, ground
- ½ teaspoon agave nectar
- A pinch of saffron
- Cooking spray

Directions:

1. Spray your air fryer with cooking spray, add milk, oats, carrots, cardamom and agave nectar, stir, cover and cook at 365°f for 15 minutes
2. Divide into bowls, sprinkle saffron on top and serve for breakfast.
3. Enjoy!

BRUNCH RECIPES

Potato and kale croquettes

Preparation Time: 5 minutes

Cooking Time: 7 minutes

Servings: 6

Ingredients

- 2 eggs, slightly beaten
- 1/3 cup flour
- 1/3 cup goat cheese, crumbled
- 1/2 tsp. fine sea salt 4 garlic cloves, minced
- 1 cup kale, steamed
- 1/3 cup breadcrumbs
- 1/3tsp. red pepper flakes
- 2 potatoes, peeled and quartered
- 1/3 tsp. dried dill weed

Directions:

1. Firstly, boil the potatoes in salted water. Once the potatoes are cooked, mash them; add the kale, goat cheese, minced garlic, sea salt, red pepper flakes, dill and one egg; stir to combine well.
2. Now, roll the mixture to form small croquettes.
3. Grab three shallow bowls. Place the flour in the first shallow bowl.
4. Beat the remaining 3 eggs in the second bowl. After that, throw the breadcrumbs into the third shallow bowl.

5. Dip each croquette in the flour; then, dip them in the eggs bowl; lastly, roll each croquette in the breadcrumbs.
6. Air fry at 335 °f for 7 minutes or until golden. Adjust for seasonings and serve warm.

Nutrition: 309 Calories; 9g Fat; 48g Carbs; 11g Protein; 2g sugars

Meat, corn and potato barbecue

Preparation time: 3 minutes

Cooking time: 27 minutes

Servings: 4

Ingredients

- 2 Pancetta belly bacon slices
- 2 sausages
- 1 corn on the cob
- 1 mealy potato
- 2 spareribs
- 2 shasliks
- Salt and pepper to taste
- Barbecue sauce

Directions:

1. Heat the air fryer to 392°f. Put the potato in it and cook for 15 minutes.
2. Put in the corn and meat-shasliks, pancetta bacons, sausages and spareribs and grill for 12 minutes.
3. Remove and sprinkle with salt and pepper. Serve with barbecue sauce and vegetable salad.

Nutrition: Calories 113 Fat 2 g Carbohydrates 3 g Sugar 2 g Protein 4 g Cholesterol 18 mg

LUNCH RECIPES

Maple mustard glazed turkey

Preparation time: 10 minutes

Cooking time: 25 minutes

Servings: 4

Ingredients:

- 1 turkey breast (about 1½2 lbs.
- 1 tbsp olive oil
- 1/4 tsp paprika
- 1/2 tsp thyme
- 1/8 tsp dry mustard
- 1/4 tsp garlic powder
- 1/2 tsp salt
- 1/4 tsp freshly ground black pepper
- 1 tbsp maple syrup
- 1 tbsp Dijon mustard
- 1 tbsp unsalted butter, melted

Directions:

1. Preheat the air fryer to 350°F.
2. Combine paprika, olive oil, thyme, dry mustard, garlic powder, salt, and freshly ground black pepper in a bowl.
3. Massage turkey breast with the oil mixture.
4. Put the turkey in the fryer basket. Cook for 15 minutes.
5. Once done, turn the turkey breast using tongs and cook for 10 minutes more.
6. Using a separate bowl, mix the maple syrup, Dijon mustard, and unsalted butter.
7. Turn the turkey breast and brush the glaze all over the turkey breast.
8. Cook for 3 minutes more.
9. Transfer to a serving plate and enjoy!

Nutrition: Calories: 350 Fat: 6g Carbs: 33g Protein: 40g Sugars: 16g Fiber: 3g

Turkey and vegetables kabobs

Preparation time: 15 minutes

Cooking time: 20 minutes

Servings: 4

Ingredients:

- 1/4 cup of soy sauce
- 1 tbsp honey
- 2 garlic cloves, minced
- 1 lb. Boneless skinless turkey breast tenderloins, cut into large chunks
- 1 large zucchini, cut into chunks
- 1 yellow bell pepper, chunks
- 1 red onion, cut into large chunks
- 1 cup cherry tomatoes
- Cooking or olive oil spray

Directions:

1. Rinse skewers in water for at 30 minutes if using wooden ones.
2. Preheat the air fryer to 350°F.
3. Place turkey, zucchini, bell pepper, onion, and tomatoes in a large bowl.
4. Using a small mixing bowl, combine soy sauce, honey, garlic, and rosemary. Mix well.
5. Pour prepared sauce over turkey and vegetables and toss to coat well.
6. Thread the turkey and vegetables onto skewers.
7. Transfer to the air fryer and spray with cooking spray.
8. Cook for 15 minutes, flipping once halfway through.
9. Transfer to the serving plates.
10. Serve and enjoy!

Nutrition: Calories: 405 Fat: 19g Carbs: 60g Protein: 7g Sugars: 41g Fiber: 9g

Turkey meatloaf

Preparation time: 15 minutes

Cooking time: 25 minutes

Servings: 4

Ingredients:

- 1 lb. 99% lean ground turkey
- 1/2 cup breadcrumbs
- 1 large egg, beaten
- 1 tbsp tomato paste
- 1/3 cup of frozen corn
- 1/4 cup onion, minced
- 1/4 cup red bell pepper, chopped
- 1/4 cup scallions, chopped
- 1 garlic clove, minced
- 2 tbsp fresh cilantro, chopped

- 1 tsp salt
- 1/2 tsp ground cumin
- 1/4 tsp chili powder
- Olive oil spray
- 2 tbsp ketchup
- 1 tsp Worcestershire sauce
- 1 tsp honey

Directions:

1. Coat the inside of a loaf pan that fits in your air fryer with cooking spray or oil. Set aside.
2. Preheat the air fryer to 350°F.
3. Prepare the turkey, breadcrumbs, egg, tomato paste, corn, onion, bell pepper scallions, garlic and fresh cilantro in large mixing bowl.
4. Season with salt, ground cumin, chili powder and gently mix until just combined.
5. Place in the prepared loaf pan.
6. Using a separate bowl, mix ketchup, Worcestershire sauce and honey.
7. Brush the meatloaves with the ketchup mixture.
8. Transfer the meatloaf to the air fryer and cook for 20 minutes.
9. Let cool for 10 minutes before slicing.
10. Transfer to a serving plate and enjoy!

Nutrition: Calories: 297 Fat: 19g Carbs: 6g Protein: 25g Sugars: 3g Fiber: 1g

Turkey cordon bleu

Preparation time: 15 minutes

Cooking time: 20 minutes

Servings: 4

Ingredients:

- 1 lb. Turkey breast
- 1 tsp salt
- 1/4 tsp thyme, dried
- 1/4 tsp freshly ground black pepper
- 1 tbsp cream cheese
- 4 slices ham
- 4 slices swiss cheese
- 1 egg, beaten
- 1/4 cup all-purpose flour
- 1 cup breadcrumbs

Directions:

1. Preheat the air fryer to 360°F.
2. Slice turkey breast into four equal pieces.

3. Pound each piece slightly with a rolling pin or the smooth side of a meat mallet or heavy skillet until they are about ½inch thick.
4. Season with salt, thyme, and pepper.
5. Lay out cream cheese evenly over one side of each piece of meat.
6. Top with ham slices and swiss cheese.
7. Roll the breast and secure with toothpicks.
8. Whisk egg in a small bowl.
9. Place flour on a shallow plate.
10. Spread breadcrumbs in a bowl.
11. Coat the cordon bleu with the flour and then dip in egg.
12. Sprinkle with breadcrumbs and place in the greased air fryer basket.
13. Cook for 20 minutes, turning once halfway through.
14. Transfer to a serving plate and remove toothpicks.
15. Serve and enjoy!

Nutrition: Calories: 208 Fat: 6g Carbs: 11g Protein: 26g Sugars: 5g Fiber: 9g

Provencal pork

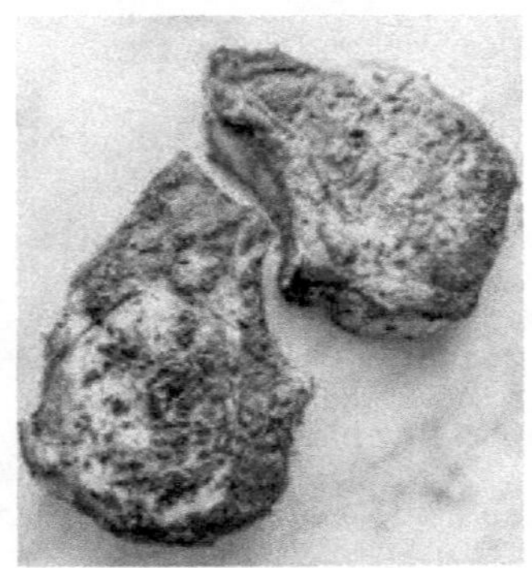

Preparation time: 10 minutes

Cooking time: 15 minutes

Servings: 2

Ingredients:

- 1, sliced red onion
- 1, cut into strips yellow bell pepper
- 1, cut into strips green bell pepper
- Salt and black pepper to taste
- 2 tsp. Provencal herbs
- 1/2 tsp. Mustard
- 1 tbsp. Olive oil
- 7 ounces pork tenderloin

Directions:

1. In a dish, mix salt, pepper, onion, green bell pepper, yellow bell pepper, half the oil, and herbs, then toss well.

2. Season pork with mustard, salt, pepper, and rest of the oil.
3. Toss well and add to veggies.
4. Cook in the air fryer at 370°F for 15 minutes. Serve.

Nutrition: Calories 300 Carbs 21g Fat 8g Protein 23g

Indian pork

Preparation time: 10 minutes

Cooking time: 12 minutes

Servings: 4

Ingredients:

- Ginger powder – 1 tsp.
- Chili paste – 2 tsp.
- Garlic cloves – 2, minced
- Pork chops – 14 ounces, cubed
- Shallot – 1, chopped
- Coriander – 1 tsp. Ground
- Coconut milk – 7 ounces
- Olive oil – 2 tbsps.
- Peanuts – 3 ounces, ground
- Soy sauce 3 tbsps.
- Salt and black pepper to taste

Directions:

1. In a bowl, mix ginger with half the oil, half of the soy sauce, half of the garlic, and 1 tsp. Chili paste.
2. Whisk and add meat. Coat and marinate for 10 minutes.
3. Cook the meat at 400°F in the air fryer for 12 minutes.
4. Meanwhile, heat the pan with the rest of the oil and add the rest of the peanuts, coconut milk, coriander, rest of the garlic, rest of the chili paste, rest of the soy sauce, and shallot.
5. Stir-fry for 5 minutes. Divide pork on plates, spread coconut mix on top, and serve.

Nutrition: Calories 423 Carbs 42g Fat 11g Protein 18g

Creamy pork

Preparation time: 10 minutes

Cooking time: 22 minutes

Servings: 6

Ingredients:

- Pork meat – 2 pounds, boneless and cubed
- Yellow onions – 2, chopped
- Olive oil – 1 tbsp.
- Garlic – 1 clove, minced
- Chicken stock – 3 cups
- Sweet paprika – 2 tbsps.
- Salt and black pepper to taste
- White flour – 2 tbsps.
- Sour cream – 1 1/2 cups
- Dill – 2 tbsp. Chopped

Directions:

1. In a pan, mix pork with oil, salt, and pepper.
2. Mix and place in the air fryer. Cook at 360°F for 7 minutes.
3. Add the sour cream, dill, flour, paprika, stock, garlic, and onion and mix.
4. Cook at 370°F for 15 minutes more. Serve.

Nutrition: Calories 300 Carbs 26g Fat 4g Protein 34g

Pork chops with onions

Preparation time:

Cooking time: 25 minutes

Servings: 2

Ingredients:

- Pork chops – 2
- Olive oil – ¼ cup
- Yellow onions – 2, sliced
- Garlic cloves – 2, minced
- Mustard – 2 tsp.
- Sweet paprika – 1 tsp.
- Salt and black pepper to taste
- Oregano – ½ tsp. Dried
- Thyme – ½ tsp. Dried
- A pinch of cayenne pepper

Directions:

1. In a bowl, mix oil with cayenne, thyme, oregano, black pepper, paprika, mustard, and garlic. Whisk well.
2. Combine onions with meat and mustard mix.
3. Mix well to coat, cover and marinate in the refrigerator for 1 day.
4. Transfer meat and onions mix to a pan and cook in the air fryer at 360F for 25 minutes. Serve.

Nutrition: Calories 384 Carbs 17g Fat 4g Protein 25g

Braised pork

Preparation time: 15 minutes

Cooking time: 40 minutes

Servings: 4

Ingredients:

- Pork loin roast – 2 pounds, boneless and cubed
- Butter – 4 tbsps. Melted
- Salt and black pepper to taste
- Chicken stock – 2 cups
- Dry white wine – ½ cup
- Garlic – 2 cloves, minced
- Thyme – 1 tsp. Chopped
- Thyme spring – 1
- Bay leaf – 1
- Yellow onion – ½, chopped
- White flour – 2 tbsps.
- Red grapes – ½ pound

Directions:

1. Season pork cubes with salt and pepper. Rub with 2 tablespoons melted butter and put in the air fryer.
2. Cook at 370°F for 8 minutes.
3. Meanwhile, heat a pan with 2 tablespoons of butter over medium heat. Put the onion and garlic—stir fry for 2 minutes.
4. Add a bay leaf, flour, thyme, salt, pepper, stock, and wine. Mix well. Bring to simmer, then remove from the heat.
5. Add grapes and pork cubes.
6. Put in the air fryer at 360°F and cook for 30 minutes. Serve.

Nutrition: Calories 320 Carbs 29g Fat 4g Protein 38g

Pork with couscous

Preparation time: 10 minutes

Cooking time: 35 minutes

Servings: 6

Ingredients:

- Pork loin – 2 1/2 pounds, boneless, and trimmed
- Chicken stock – 3/4 cup
- Olive oil – 2 tbsps.
- Sweet paprika – 1/2 tbsp.
- Dried sage – 2 1/4 tsps.
- Garlic powder – 1/2 tsp.
- Dried rosemary – 1/4 tsp.
- Dried marjoram – 1/4 tsp.
- Dried basil – 1 tsp.
- Dried oregano – 1 tsp.
- Salt and black pepper to taste
- Couscous – 2 cups, cooked

Directions:

1. In a bowl, mix oil with stock, salt, pepper, oregano, marjoram, thyme, rosemary, sage, garlic powder, and paprika.
2. Whisk well and add pork loin. Mix and marinate for 1 hour.
3. Cook in the air fryer at 370°F for 35 minutes.
4. Divide among plates and serve with couscous on the side.

Nutrition: Calories 310 Carbs 37g Fat 4g Protein 34g

Pulled pork

Preparation time: 10 minutes

Cooking time: 2 hours and 30 minutes

Servings: 8

Ingredients:

- Chili powder – 2 tbsps.
- Garlic powder – 1 tsp.
- Onion powder – 1/2 tsp.
- Ground black pepper – 1/2 tsp.
- Cumin – 1/2 tsp.
- Pork shoulder – 1 (4pound

Directions:

1. In a bowl, mix cumin, pepper, onion powder, garlic powder, and chili powder.
2. Put the spice mixture over the pork shoulder.
3. Place the pork shoulder into the air fryer basket.

4. Cook at 350F for 150 minutes.
5. Shred the meat with forks and serve.

Nutrition: Calories 537 Carbs 1g Fat 35g Protein 43g

Juicy pork chops

Preparation time: 10 minutes

Cooking time: 15 minutes

Servings: 2

Ingredients:

- Chili powder – 1 tsp.
- Garlic powder – 1/2 tsp.
- Cumin – 1/2 tsp.
- Ground black pepper – 1/4 tsp.
- Dried oregano – 1/4 tsp.
- Boneless pork chops – 2 (4ounce
- Unsalted butter – 2 tbsps. Divided

Directions:

1. Mix oregano, pepper, cumin, garlic powder, and chili powder in a bowl. Rub dry rub onto pork chops.

2. Add pork chops into the air fryer basket.
3. Cook at 400°F for 15 minutes.
4. Serve each chop topped with 1 tbsp. Butter.

Nutrition: Calories 313 Carbs 1g Fat 26g Protein 24g

Pork salad

Preparation time: 10 minutes

Cooking time: 8 minutes

Servings: 2

Ingredients:

- Coconut oil – 1 tbsp.
- Pork chops – 2 (4ouncechopped into 1inch cubes
- Chili powder – 2 tsp.
- Paprika – 1 tsp.
- Garlic powder – 1/2 tsp.
- Onion powder – 1/4 tsp.
- Chopped romaine – 4 cups
- Roma tomato – 1 medium, diced
- Shredded Monterey jack cheese – 1/2 cup
- Avocado – 1, diced
- Full fat ranch dressing – 1/4 cup
- Chopped cilantro – 1 tbsp.

Directions:

1. Drizzle coconut oil over the pork and sprinkle with onion powder, garlic powder, paprika, and chili powder.
2. Place pork into the air fryer basket. Cook at 400°F for 8 minutes.
3. In a bowl, place crispy pork, tomato, and romaine. Top with shredded cheese and avocado.
4. Pour ranch dressing around the bowl and toss to coat. Top with cilantro. Serve.

Nutrition: Calories 526 Carbs 2g Fat 37g Protein 34g

Beef with peas and mushrooms

Preparation time: 10 minutes

Cooking time: 22 minutes

Servings: 2

Ingredients:

- Beef steaks – 2, cut into strips
- Salt and black pepper to taste
- Snow peas – 7 ounces
- White mushrooms – 8 ounces, halved
- Yellow onion – 1, cut into rings
- Soy sauce – 2 tbsps.
- Olive oil – 1 tsp.

Directions:

1. In a bowl, mix soy sauce and olive oil, and whisk. Add beef strips and coat.

2. In another bowl, mix mushrooms, onion, snow peas with salt, pepper, and the oil. Toss well.
3. Place in pan and cook in the air fryer at 350°F for 16 minutes.
4. Add beef strips to the pan as well and cook at 400°F for 6 minutes more. Serve.

Nutrition: Calories 235 Carbs 22g Fat 8g Protein 24g

DINNER RECIPES

Roast chicken

Preparation time: 10 minutes

Cooking time: 50 minutes

Servings: 8

Ingredients:

- 1 whole chicken
- Chicken dry rub
- Cooking spray

Directions:

1. Spray chicken with oil.
2. Sprinkle with the dry rub.
3. Roast the chicken in the air fryer at 330 °F for 30 minutes.
4. Turn and roast for another 20 minutes.

Nutrition: Calories: 166 Fat: 6g Carbs: 1g Protein: 25g

General Tso's chicken

Preparation time: 20 minutes

Cooking time: 35 minutes

Servings: 4

Ingredients:

- 1 lb. Chicken thigh fillets, sliced into smaller pieces
- Salt and pepper to taste
- 1 egg, beaten
- ¼ cup cornstarch
- Sauce
- 2 tablespoons reduced sodium soy sauce
- 1 ½ tablespoon vegetable oil
- 2 teaspoons rice vinegar
- 8 tablespoons chicken broth
- 2 teaspoons sugar
- 2 tablespoons ketchup
- 3 chiles de árbol, chopped and seeded

- 1 clove garlic, minced
- 1 tablespoon ginger, chopped

Directions:

1. Season chicken with salt and pepper.
2. Dip in egg and coat with cornstarch.
3. Set the air fryer at 400 °F and cook for 15 minutes, flipping once or twice.
4. In a pan over medium heat, simmer sauce ingredients for 15 minutes.
5. Add chicken to the pan.
6. Mix well.
7. Cook for 5 minutes.
8. Serve warm.

Nutrition: Calories: 397 Fat: 9g Carbs: 29g Protein: 46g

Buttermilk fried chicken

Preparation time: 8 hours

Cooking time: 45 minutes

Servings: 6

Ingredients:

- Marinade
- 2 lb. Chicken
- 1 cup buttermilk
- ¼ cup hot sauce
- 1 teaspoon paprika
- 1 teaspoon garlic powder
- Salt and pepper to taste
- Breading
- 1 cup flour
- 1 teaspoon garlic powder
- 1 teaspoon paprika
- ½ cup cornstarch

- Salt and pepper to taste
- Cooking spray

Directions:

1. Mix the marinade ingredients in a bowl.
2. Cover and refrigerate for 8 hours.
3. Warm your air fryer to 375 °F.
4. In a bowl, mix the breading ingredients.
5. Add 2 tablespoons buttermilk batter to the flour bowl and mix well.
6. Dredge chicken with flour mixture.
7. Cook the chicken for 30 minutes.
8. Flip and cook for 15 minutes.

Nutrition: Calories: 335**:** Fat: 13g Carbs: 33g Protein: 24g

SIDE DISH RECIPES

Easy frizzled leeks

Preparation Time: 25 minutes

Cooking Time: 18 minutes

Servings 6

Ingredients

- 1/2 teaspoon porcini powder
- 1 1/2 cup rice flour
- 1 tablespoon vegetable oil
- 3 medium-sized leeks, slice into julienne strips
- 2 large-sized dishes with ice water
- 2 teaspoons onion powder
- Fine sea salt and cayenne pepper, to taste

Directions

1. Allow the leeks to soak in ice water for about 25 minutes; drain well.
2. Place the rice flour, salt, cayenne pepper, onions powder, and porcini powder into a resealable bag. Add the celery and shake to coat well.
3. Drizzle vegetable oil over the seasoned leeks. Air fry at 390 °F for about 18 minutes; turn them halfway through the cooking time. Serve with homemade mayonnaise or any other sauce for dipping. Enjoy!

Nutrition:291 calories; 6g fat; 53g carbs; 7g protein; 3g sugars

Oyster mushroom and lemongrass omelet

Preparation Time: 7 minutes

Cooking Time: 35 minutes

Servings 2

Ingredients

- 3 king oyster mushrooms, thinly sliced
- 1 lemongrass, chopped
- 1/2 teaspoon dried marjoram
- 5 eggs
- 1/3 cup swiss cheese, grated
- 2 tablespoons sour cream
- 1 1/2 teaspoon dried rosemary
- 2 teaspoons red pepper flakes, crushed
- 2 tablespoons butter, melted
- 1/2 red onion, peeled and sliced into thin rounds
- ½ teaspoon garlic powder
- 1 teaspoon dried dill weed
- Fine sea salt and ground black pepper, to your liking

Directions

1. Get the onion then peeled and sliced into thin rounds
2. Melt the margarine in a skillet that is placed over a medium flame. Then, sweat the onion, mushrooms, and lemongrass until they have softened; reserve.

3 Then, preheat the air fryer to 325° F. Then, crack the eggs into a mixing bowl and whisk them well. Then, fold in the sour cream and give it a good stir.

4 Now, stir in the salt, black pepper, red pepper, rosemary, garlic powder, marjoram, and dill.

5 Grease the inside of an air fryer baking dish with a thin layer of a cooking spray. Pour the egg/seasoning mixture into the baking dish; throw in the reserved mixture. Top with the Swiss cheese.

6 Set the timer for 35 minutes; cook until a knife inserted in the center comes out clean and dry

Nutrition:362 calories; 29g fat; 2g carbs; 19g protein; 8g sugars

CASSEROLES

Cheesy sausage and broccoli casserole

Preparation time: 10 minutes

Cooking time: 20 minutes

Servings: 8

Ingredients:

- 10 eggs
- 1 cup cheddar cheese, shredded and divided
- ¾ cup heavy whipping cream
- 1 (12ounce / 340g package cooked chicken sausage
- 1 cup broccoli, chopped
- 2 cloves garlic, minced
- ½ tablespoon salt
- ¼ tablespoon ground black pepper
- Cooking spray

Directions:

1. Spritz a baking pan with cooking spray.
2. Whisk the eggs with cheddar and cream in a large bowl to mix well.

3. Combine the cooked sausage, broccoli, salt, garlic, and ground black pepper in a separate bowl. Stir to mix well.
4. Put sausage mixture into the baking pan, then spread the egg mixture over to cover.
5. Put the baking pan in the air fryer. Cook at the corresponding preset mode or air fry at 400°F (204°C until the eggs are set).
6. Serve immediately.

Nutrition: Calories: 370 Fat: 20g Carbs: 32g Protein: 17g

CHICKEN AND POULTRY

Zucchini Stuffed Lemony Chicken

Preparation Time: 20 minutes

Cooking time: 2 hours

Servings: 6

Ingredients:

- 1 whole chicken, 3 lb.
- 2 red and peeled onions
- 2 tbsp olive oil
- 2 apricots
- 1 zucchini
- 1 apple
- 2 cloves finely chopped garlic
- Fresh chopped thyme
- Salt and black pepper to taste
- 5 oz honey
- juice from 1 lemon
- 2 tbsp olive oil
- Salt and black pepper to taste

Directions:

1. For the stuffing, chop all Ingredients: into tiny pieces. Transfer to a large bowl and add the olive oil. Season with salt and black pepper. Fill the cavity of the chicken with the stuffing, without packing it tightly.

2. Place the chicken in the Air Fryer and cook for 35 minutes at 340 F. Warm the honey and the lemon juice in a large pan; season with salt and pepper. Reduce the temperature of the Air Fryer to 320 F.
3. Brush the chicken with some of the honey-lemon marinade and return it to the fryer. Cook for another 70 minutes; brush the chicken every 20-25 minutes with the marinade. Garnish with parsley and serve with potatoes.

Nutrition: Calories: 179 Fat: 4g Carbs: 21g Protein: 19g

Drumsticks with Blue Cheese Sauce

Preparation Time: 2 hours

Cooking time: 25 minutes

Servings: 4

Ingredients:

- 1 lb. mini drumsticks
- 3 tbsp butter
- 3 tbsp paprika
- 2 tbsp powdered cumin
- ¼ cup hot sauce
- 1 tbsp maple syrup
- 2 tbsp onion powder
- 2 tbsp garlic powder
- ½ cup mayonnaise
- 1 cup crumbled blue cheese
- 1 cup sour cream
- 1 ½ tbsp garlic powder
- 1 ½ tbsp onion powder
- Salt and black pepper to taste
- 1 ½ tbsp cayenne pepper
- 1 ½ tbsp white wine vinegar
- 2 tbsp buttermilk
- 1 ½ Worcestershire sauce

Directions:

1. Start with the drumstick sauce; place a pan over medium heat on a stove top. Melt the butter, and add the hot sauce, paprika, garlic, onion, maple syrup, and cumin; mix well. Cook the mixture for 5 minutes or until the sauce reduces. Turn off the heat and let cool. Put the drumsticks in a bowl, pour half of the sauce over, and mix it.
2. Save the remaining sauce for serving. Refrigerate the drumsticks for 2 hours. Meanwhile, make the blue cheese sauce: in a jug, add the sour cream, blue cheese, mayonnaise, garlic powder, onion powder, buttermilk, cayenne pepper, vinegar, Worcestershire sauce, pepper, and salt. Using a stick blender, blend the Ingredients: until they are well mixed with no large lumps. Adjust the salt and pepper taste as desired. Preheat the Air Fryer to 350° F.
3. Remove the drumsticks from the fridge and place them in the fryer basket; cook for 15 minutes. Turn the drumsticks with tongs every 5 minutes to ensure that they are evenly cooked. Remove the drumsticks to a serving bowl and pour the remaining sauce over. Serve with the blue cheese sauce and a side of celery sticks.

Nutrition: Calories: 210 Fat: 13g Carbs: 1g Protein: 22g

Chili Lime Chicken Lollipop

Preparation Time: 15 minutes

Cooking time: 10 minutes

Servings: 3

Ingredients:

- 1 lb. mini chicken drumsticks
- ½ tbsp soy sauce
- 1 tbsp lime juice
- Salt and black pepper to taste
- 1 tbsp cornstarch
- ½ tbsp minced garlic
- ½ tbsp chili powder
- ½ tbsp chopped cilantro
- ½ tbsp garlic-ginger paste
- 1 tbsp vinegar
- 1 tbsp chili paste
- ½ tbsp beaten egg
- 1 tbsp paprika
- 1 tbsp flour
- 2 tbsp maple syrup

Directions:

1. Mix garlic ginger paste, chili powder, maple syrup, paprika powder, chopped coriander, plain vinegar, egg, garlic, and salt, in a bowl.

2. Add the chicken drumsticks and toss to coat; Stir in cornstarch, flour, and lime juice.
3. Preheat the Air Fryer to 350° F. Remove each drumstick, shake off the excess marinade, and place in a single layer in the basket; cook for 5 minutes.
4. Slide out the basket, spray the chicken with cooking spray and continue to cook for 5 minutes. Remove onto a serving platter and serve with tomato dip and a side of steamed asparagus.

Nutrition: Calories: 150 Fat: 5g Carbs: 1g Protein: 25g

Almond Turkey with Lemon and Eggs

Preparation Time: 15 minutes

Cooking time: 35 minutes

Servings: 3

Ingredients:

- 1 lb. turkey breasts
- Salt and black pepper to taste to season
- ¼ cup chicken soup cream
- ¼ cup mayonnaise
- 2 tbsp lemon juice
- ¼ cup slivered almonds, chopped
- ¼ cup breadcrumbs
- 2 tbsp chopped green onion
- 2 tbsp chopped pimentos
- 2 Boiled eggs, chopped
- ½ cup diced celery

Directions:

1. Preheat the Air Fryer to 390° F. Place the turkey breasts on a clean flat surface and season with salt and pepper.
2. Grease with cooking spray and place them in the fryer's basket; cook for 13 minutes. Remove turkey back onto the chopping board, let cool, and cut into dices. In a bowl, add the celery, chopped eggs, pimentos, green onions, slivered almonds, lemon juice, mayonnaise, diced turkey, and chicken soup cream and mix well.

3. Grease a 5 X 5 inches casserole dish with cooking spray, scoop the turkey mixture into the bowl, sprinkle the breadcrumbs on it, and spray with cooking spray. Put the dish in the fryer basket and bake the Ingredients: at 390° F for 20 minutes. Remove and serve with a side of steamed asparagus.

Nutrition: Calories: 214 Fat: 6g Carbs: 18g Protein: 21g

BEEF, STEAK AND LAMB RECIPES

Rib Eye Steak

Preparation Time: 5 minutes

Cooking Time: 15-20 minutes

Servings: 4

Ingredients

- 2 pounds rib eye steak
- 1 tablespoon steak rub
- 1 tablespoon olive oil

Directions

1. Preheat your Air Fryer to 390-400° F.
2. Season the steak on both sides with rub and sprinkle with olive oil.
3. Cook the steak for about 7-8 minutes, rotate the steak and cook for another 6-7 minute until golden brown and ready.

Nutrition: Calories: 360 Fat: 32g Carbs: 0g Protein: 18g

Fried Beef with Potatoes and Mushrooms

Preparation Time: 20 minutes

Cooking Time: 15 minutes

Servings: 3

Ingredients

- 1-pound beef steak
- 1 medium onion, sliced
- 8 oz mushrooms, sliced
- ½ pound potatoes, diced
- Sauce you prefer (Barbecue or Teriyaki)
- Salt and black pepper for seasoning

Directions

1. Wash vegetables, chop onion and mushrooms, dice potatoes.
2. Sprinkle them with salt and pepper.
3. Cut beef steak into 1-inch pieces.
4. In the large mixing bowl combine onion, potatoes, mushrooms and beef. Marinate with sauce and set aside for 15-20 minutes.
5. Preheat the Air Fryer to 350-370°F
6. Put meat and vegetables into the Fryer and cook for 15 minutes.
7. After cooking replace the meal to the serving plate and sprinkle with fresh chopped parsley.

Nutrition: Calories: 336 Fat: 16g Carbs: 22g Protein: 25g

FISH AND SEAFOODS

Bacon-wrapped shrimp

Preparation time: 5 minutes

Cooking time: 5 minutes

servings: 4

Ingredients

- 1¼ pound tiger shrimp, peeled and deveined
- Pound bacon

Directions:

1. Preparing the ingredients. Wrap each shrimp with a slice of bacon.
2. Refrigerate for about 20 minutes.
3. Preheat the air fryer oven to 390° f.
4. Air frying. Arrange the shrimp in the oven rack/basket. Place the rack on the middle-shelf of the air fryer oven. Cook for about 5-7 minutes.

Nutrition: Calories 70 Total fat 5g Total carbs 0g Fiber 0g Protein 7g Sugar 0g Sodium 150mg

Fried scallops with saffron cream sauce

Preparation time: 5 minutes;

Cooking time: 2 minutes;

Servings: 4

Ingredients:

- Olive oil for greasing
- 24 scallops, cleaned
- 2/3 cup heavy cream
- Tbsp freshly squeezed lemon juice
- ¼ tsp dried crushed saffron threads

Directions:

1. Insert the dripping pan in the bottom part of the air fryer and preheat the oven at air fry mode 400° f for 2 to 3 minutes.
2. Lightly brush the rotisserie basket with some olive oil and fill with the scallops.
3. Close and fit the basket in the oven using the rotisserie lift and set the timer for 2 minutes or until the scallops are golden brown on the outside.
4. Meanwhile, in a medium bowl, quickly whisk the heavy cream lemon juice and saffron threads.
5. When the scallops are ready, transfer to a serving plate and drizzle the sauce on top.
6. Enjoy immediately.

Nutrition: Calories 77, total fat 73g, total carbs 05g, fiber 0g, protein 15g, sugar 66g, sodium 31mg

FRUIT AND VEGETABLES

Sesame broccoli mix

Preparation time: 5 minutes

Cooking time: 14 minutes

Servings: 4

Ingredients:

- 1pound broccoli florets
- 1 tablespoon sesame oil
- 1 teaspoon sesame seeds, toasted
- 1 red onion, sliced
- 1 tablespoon lime juice
- 1 teaspoon chili powder
- Salt and black pepper to the taste

Directions:

1. In your air fryer, combine the broccoli with the oil, sesame seeds and the other ingredients, toss and cook at 380° f for 14 minutes.
2. Divide between plates and serve.

Nutrition: calories 141, fat 3, fiber 4, carbohydrates 4, protein 2

Cabbage sauté

Preparation time: 5 minutes

Cooking time: 15 minutes

Servings: 4

Ingredients:

- 1pound red cabbage, shredded
- 1 tablespoon balsamic vinegar
- 2 red onions, sliced
- 1 tablespoon olive oil
- 1 tablespoon dill, chopped
- Salt and black pepper to the taste

Directions:

1. Heat up air fryer with oil at 380° f, add the cabbage, onions and the other ingredients, toss and cook for 15 minutes.
2. Divide between plates and serve.

Nutrition: calories 100, fat 4, fiber 2, carbohydrates 7, protein 2

SNACK RECIPES

Blueberry Pudding

Preparation Time: 15 minutes

Cooking Time: 35 minutes

Servings: 6

Ingredients:

- 3 Tablespoons Maple syrup
- 2 Tablespoons Rosemary, Fresh & Chopped
- 2 Cups Flour
- 2 Cups Rolled Oats
- 8 Cups Blueberries, fresh
- 1 Stick Butter, Melted
- 1 Cup Walnuts, Chopped

Directions:

1. Start by spreading your blueberries in a greased pan that fits in your air fryer.
2. Get out a food processor and mix your flour, walnuts, butter, oats, maple syrup and rosemary. Blend well, and then place this over your blueberries.
3. Cook at 350°f for twenty-five minutes. Allow it to cool before slicing to serve.

Nutrition: Calories: 150 Protein: 4g Fat: 3g Carbs: 7g

Green Sandwich

Preparation Time: 15 minutes

Cooking Time: 10 to 13 minutes

Servings 4

Ingredients:

- 1½ cups chopped mixed greens
- 2 garlic cloves, thinly sliced
- 2 teaspoons olive oil
- 2 slices low sodium Swiss cheese
- 4 slices low sodium whole wheat bread
- Cooking spray

Directions:

1. In a nonstick round baking pan, mix the greens, garlic, and olive oil.
2. Detach the rotating blade of the air fryer and slide the baking pan into the air fryer. Cook at the corresponding preset mode or Air Fry at 400°f (204° C) for 4 to 5 minutes. Stirring once, until the vegetables are tender. Drain, if necessary.
3. Make 2 sandwiches, dividing half of the greens and 1 slice of Swiss cheese between 2 slices of bread. Lightly spray the outsides of the sandwiches with cooking spray.
4. Cook at the corresponding preset mode or bake the sandwiches in the air fryer for 6 to 8 minutes, turning with tongs halfway through, until the bread is toasted and the cheese melts.
5. Cut each sandwich in half and serve.

Nutrition: Calories: 245 Fat: 2g Carbs: 28g Protein: 8g

Eggplant Sandwich

Preparation Time: 10 minutes

Cooking Time: 9 to 12 minutes

Servings 4

Ingredients:

- 1 baby eggplant, peeled and chopped
- 1 red bell pepper, sliced
- ½ cup diced red onion
- ½ cup shredded carrot
- 1 teaspoon olive oil
- 1/3 cup Greek yogurt
- ½ teaspoon dried tarragon
- 2 lows odium whole wheat pita breads, halved crosswise

Directions:

1. Stir together the eggplant, red bell pepper, red onion, carrot, and olive oil in the air fryer basket. Cook at the corresponding preset mode or Air Fry at 390°F (199°C) for 7 to 9 minutes or until the vegetables are tender. Drain if necessary.
2. In a small bowl, carefully mix the yogurt and tarragon until well combined.
3. Stir the yogurt mixture into the vegetables. Stuff one fourth of this mixture into each pita pocket.
4. Detach the rotating blade of the air fryer basket and place the sandwiches in. Cook at the corresponding preset mode or bake for 2 to

3 minutes, or until the bread is toasted. Flip the sandwiches halfway through.

5. Serve immediately.

Nutrition: Calories: 423 Fat: 18g Carbs: 42g Protein: 22g

Bacon Sandwich

Preparation Time: 10 minutes

Cooking Time: 6 minutes

Servings 4

Ingredients:

- 1/3 cup spicy barbecue sauce
- 2 tablespoons honey
- 8 slices cooked bacon, cut into thirds
- 1 red bell pepper, sliced
- 1 yellow bell pepper, sliced
- 3 pita pockets, cut in half
- 1¼ cups torn butter lettuce leaves
- 2 tomatoes, sliced

Directions:

1. In a small bowl, put the barbecue sauce and the honey. Brush this mixture lightly onto the bacon slices and the red and yellow pepper slices.
2. Put the peppers into the air fryer basket. Cook at the corresponding preset mode or Air Fry at 350° F (177° C) for 4 minutes.
3. Add the bacon, and Air Fry for 2 more minutes or until the bacon is browned and the peppers are tender.
4. Fill the pita with the bacon, peppers, any remaining barbecue sauce, lettuce, and tomatoes, and serve immediately.

Nutrition: Calories: 450 Fat: 29g Carbs: 26g Protein: 20g

Tuna Sandwich

Preparation Time: 8 minutes

Cooking Time: 4 to 8 minutes

Servings 4

Ingredients:

- 1 can chunk light tuna, drained
- ¼ cup mayonnaise
- 2 tablespoons mustard
- 1 tablespoon lemon juice
- 2 green onions, minced
- 4 slices of whole or wheat bread
- 3 tablespoons softened butter
- 6 thin slices cheese

Directions:

1. Put together the tuna, mayonnaise, mustard, lemon juice, and green onions. Set aside.
2. Arrange the bread, butter side up, in the air fryer.
3. Cook at 390° F (199° C) for 2 to 4 minutes, or until golden brown.
4. Put one slice of cheese on top of each bread and return to the air fryer. Cook until the cheese melts and starts to brown.
5. Take out from the air fryer, top with the tuna mixture, and serve.

Nutrition: Calories: 240 Fat: 5g Carbs: 27g Protein: 25g

APPETIZER RECIPES

Arancini

Preparation time: 15 minutes

cooking time: 16 to 22 minutes

servings: 16 arancini

Ingredients:

- 2 cups cooked and cooled rice or leftover risotto
- 2 eggs, beaten
- 1½ cups panko breadcrumbs, divided
- ½ cup grated parmesan cheese
- 2 tablespoons minced fresh basil
- 16 ¾-inch cubes mozzarella cheese
- 2 tablespoons olive oil

Directions:

1. in a medium bowl, combine the rice, eggs, ½ cup of the breadcrumbs, parmesan cheese, and basil. Form this mixture into 16 1½-inch balls.
2. poke a hole in each of the balls with your finger and insert a mozzarella cube. Form the rice mixture firmly around the cheese.
3. on a shallow plate, combine the remaining 1 cup breadcrumbs with the olive oil and mix well. Roll the rice balls in the breadcrumbs to coat.
4. cook the arancini in batches for 8 to 11 minutes or until golden brown.

Nutrition (2 arancini: calories: 378; total fat: 11g; saturated fat: 4g; cholesterol: 57mg; sodium: 361mg; carbohydrates: 53g; fiber: 2g; protein: 16g

PASTA AND RICE RECIPES

Chicken and Broccoli Rice

Preparation Time: 5 minutes

Cooking Time: 20 minutes

Servings 4 to 6

Ingredients:

- 2 tablespoons butter
- 2 cloves garlic, minced
- 1 onion, chopped
- 1½ pounds (680 g) boneless chicken breasts, sliced
- Salt and ground black pepper, to taste
- 11/3 cups chicken broth
- 11/3 cups long grain rice
- ½ cup milk
- 1 cup broccoli florets
- ½ cup grated Cheddar cheese

Directions:

1. Set your Instant Pot to Sauté and melt the butter.
2. Add the garlic, onion, and chicken pieces to the pot. Season with salt and pepper to taste.
3. Sauté for 5 minutes, stirring occasionally, or until the chicken is lightly browned.
4. Stir in the chicken broth, rice, milk, broccoli, and cheese.

5. Cook for 15 minutes at High Pressure.
6. When the timer beeps, perform a natural pressure release for 10 minutes, then release any remaining pressure. Carefully remove the lid.
7. Divide into bowls and serve.

Nutrition: Calories: 249 Fat: 5g Carbs: 23g Protein: 0g

BREAD & GRAINS

Asian-style shrimp pilaf

Preparation Time: 15 minutes

Cooking Time: 45 minutes

Servings: 3

Ingredients

- 1 cup koshihikari rice, rinsed
- 1 yellow onion, chopped
- 2 garlic cloves, minced
- 1/2 teaspoon fresh ginger, grated
- 1 tablespoon shoyu sauce
- 2 tablespoons rice wine
- 1 tablespoon sushi seasoning
- 1 tablespoon caster sugar
- 1/2 teaspoon sea salt
- 5 ounces frozen shrimp, thawed
- 2 tablespoons katsuobushi flakes, for serving

Directions

1. Place the koshihikari rice and 2 cups of water in a large saucepan and bring to a boil. Cover turn the heat down to low and continue cooking for 15 minutes more. Set aside for 10 minutes.
2. Mix the rice, onion, garlic, ginger, shoyu sauce, wine, sushi seasoning, sugar, and salt in a lightly greased baking dish.

3. Cook in the preheated air fryer at 370°f for 13 to 16 minutes.
4. Add the shrimp to the baking dish and gently stir until everything is well combined. Cook for 6 minutes more.
5. Serve at room temperature, garnished with katsuobushi flakes. Enjoy!

Nutrition: 368 calories; 3g fat; 64g carbs; 9g protein; 19g sugars

DESSERT RECIPES

Cream Cheese Muffins

Preparation Time: 15 minutes

Cooking time: 10 minutes

Servings: 8

Ingredients:

- 1 egg
- 1 cup cream cheese
- 1 cup almond flour
- ¼ teaspoon salt
- 1 teaspoon baking soda
- 1 teaspoon apple cider vinegar
- teaspoon swerves
- 2 tablespoon coconut flakes

Directions:

1 Break egg in a bowl and add cream cheese.
2 Whisk the mixture well.
3 Sprinkle the cream cheese mixture with the almond flour, salt, baking soda, and apple cider vinegar.
4 Add swerve and coconut flakes.
5 Use a hand mixer to make the dough.
6 Preheat the air fryer to 360° F.

7. Fill 1/2 part of every muffin mold with the muffin dough and put the muffins in the air fryer.
8. Cook for 10 minutes.
9. Allow to cool before serving.

Nutrition: calories 135, fat 12.8, fiber 0.5, carbs 2.3, protein 3.7

Tangerine Cake

Preparation Time: 10 minutes

Cooking Time: 20 minutes

Servings: 8

Ingredients:

- ¾ cup sugar 2 cups flour
- ¼ cup olive oil
- ½ cup milk
- 1 teaspoon juice vinegar
- ½ teaspoon vanilla concentrate
- Juice and get-up-and-go from 2 lemons
- Juice and get-up-and-go from 1 tangerine
- Tangerine slices, for serving

Directions:

1 In a bowl, blend flour in with sugar and mix.

2 In another bowl, blend oil in with milk, vinegar, vanilla concentrate, lemon squeeze and pizzazz and tangerine get-up-and-go and whisk quite well.

3 Add flour, mix well, empty this into a cake skillet that accommodates the air fryer cooker, present in the fryer and cook at 360°F for about 20 minutes.

4 Serve immediately with tangerine slices on top. Enjoy the recipe!

Nutrition: calories 190, fat 1, fiber 1, carbs 4, protein 4

Mandarin Pudding

Preparation Time: 20 minutes

Cooking Time: 40 minutes

Servings: 8

Ingredients:

- 1 mandarin, stripped and cut Juice from 2 mandarins
- 1 tablespoon darker sugar 4 ounces margarine, delicate
- 2 eggs, whisked
- ¾ cup sugar
- ¾ cup white flour
- ¾ cup almonds, ground Honey for serving

Directions:

1 Grease a portion skillet with some margarine, sprinkle dark colored sugar on the base and mastermind mandarin cuts.

2 In a bowl, blend spread in with sugar, eggs, almonds, flour and mandarin juice, mix, spoon this over mandarin cuts, place container in the air fryer cooker and cook at 360 Deg. Fahrenheit for about 40 minutes.

3 Transfer pudding to a plate and present with honey on top.

4 Enjoy the recipe!

Nutrition: calories 162, fat 3, fiber 2, carbs 3, protein 6

Cocoa and Almonds Bars

Preparation Time: 30 minutes

Cooking Time: 4 minutes

Servings: 6

Ingredients:

- ¼ cup cocoa nibs
- 1 cup almonds, drenched and depleted
- 2 tablespoons cocoa powder
- ¼ cup hemp seeds
- ¼ cup goji berries
- ¼ cup coconut, destroyed
- dates, hollowed and drenched

Directions:

1 Put almonds in your food processor, mix, include hemp seeds, cocoa nibs, cocoa powder, goji, coconut and mix quite well.

2 Add dates, mix well once more, spread on a lined heating sheet that accommodates the air fryer cooker and cook at 320 °F for about 4 minutes.

3 Cut into two halves and keep in the cooler for 30 minutes before serving.

4 Enjoy the recipe!

Nutrition: calories 140, fat 6, fiber 3, carbs 7, protein 19

Dark Colored Butter Cookies

Preparation Time: 10 minutes

Cooking Time: 10 minutes

Servings: 6

Ingredients:

- 1 and ½ cups spread
- 2 cups dark colored sugar
- 2 eggs, whisked
- cups flour
- 2/3 cup walnuts, hacked
- 2 teaspoons vanilla concentrate
- 1 teaspoon preparing pop
- ½ teaspoon preparing powder

Directions:

1 Heat up a dish with the spread over medium heat, mix until it liquefies, include dark colored sugar and mix until this disintegrates.
2 In a bowl, blend flour in with walnuts, vanilla concentrate, preparing pop, heating powder and eggs and mix well.
3 Add dark colored margarine, mix well and organize spoonful of this blend on a lined heating sheet that accommodates the air fryer cooker.
4 Introduce in the fryer and cook at 340°F for about 10 minutes.
5 Leave cookies to chill off and serve. Enjoy the recipe!

Nutrition: calories 144, fat 5, fiber 6, carbs 19, protein 2

Tomato Cake

Preparation Time: 10 minutes

Cooking Time: 30 minutes

Servings: 4

Ingredients:

1 and ½ cups flour

- 1 teaspoon cinnamon powder
- 1 teaspoon preparing powder
- 1 teaspoon preparing pop
- ¾ cup maple syrup
- 1 cup tomatoes hacked
- ½ cup olive oil
- 2 tablespoon apple juice vinegar

Directions:

1 1.In a bowl, blend flour in with preparing powder, heating pop, cinnamon and maple syrup and mix well.

1. In another bowl, blend tomatoes in with olive oil and vinegar and mix well.
2. Combine the 2 blends, mix well, fill a lubed round skillet that accommodates the air fryer cooker, present in the fryer and cook at 360°F for about 30 minutes.
3. Leave cake to chill off, cut and serve.

2 Enjoy the recipe!

Nutrition: calories 153, fat 2, fiber 1, carbs 25, protein 4

Cashew Bars

Preparation Time: 10 minutes

Cooking Time: 15 minutes

Servings: 6

Ingredients:

- 1/3 cup honey
- ¼ cup almond meal
- 1 tablespoon almond spread
- 1 and ½ cups cashews, hacked
- dates, slashed
- ¾ cup coconut, destroyed
- 1 tablespoon chia seeds

Directions:

1. In a bowl, blend honey in with almond meal and almond spread and mix well.
2. Add cashews, coconut, dates and chia seeds and mix well once more.
3. Spread this on a lined heating sheet that accommodates the air fryer cooker and press well.
4. Introduce in the fryer and cook at 300°F for about 15 minutes.
5. Leave blend to chill off, cut into medium bars and serve. Enjoy!

Nutrition: calories 121, fat 4, fiber 7, carbs 5, protein 6

CONCLUSION

Thank you for reading all this book!

Air fryers are very inexpensive. No matter what your budget is, there is an air fryer that fits it. They're mainly used for snacks. However, you can use the air fryer for other recipes if you want. They're a great alternative to the waffle iron, and you can cook a wide range of foods with them.

You have already taken a step towards your improvement.

Best wishes!

CPSIA information can be obtained
at www.ICGtesting.com
Printed in the USA
BVHW051123060321
601818BV00011BA/1525

9 781801 796729